Published 2008
ck-in-Elmet Historical Society, 2008
N 978-1-952057-23-6

## Acknowledgements

Twenty two years ago the Society published a collection of photographs of the village of Barwick-in-Elmet entitled *Bygone Barwick* .This was an instant success and a second publication is long overdue. In this publication we have included photographs from the whole of the ancient parish of Barwick-in-Elmet.

So many people have been involved in the preparation of this book that it is impossible to name everyone individually. However, we would like to thank the following who have loaned photographs, supplied names and dates etc.

Michael and David Teal, Mavis Edwards, The Kemp Family, S Banks, John Collett, Alan and Evelyn Senior, Arthur Bantoft, Freda Hewitt, Jane Deacon, Mary Eaton, Frank Noble, Dorothy Hague, Glenys Day, Pat Holmes, Sue Murray Jackie Pinkney, Margaret Lloyd, Alistair and Carol Hamilton, Betty Marson, Michelle Lefevre and staff at the Local Studies Library, Leeds. Members of Barwick-in-Elmet Historical Society and residents of Barwick-in-Elmet, Scholes, and Stanks.

Finally a special thank you to members of the Editorial Committee, Tony Cox, Hugh Hawkins, Harold Smith, and Martin Tarpey whose enthusiasm and encouragement finally brought this publication to fruition.

Pauline Robson
October 2008

### Front Cover photograph

The lady on the front cover is Mrs Martha Emmery wife of Edward Emmery. Originally from Dudley in Staffordshire, Martha was living with her husband, a miner, in Austhorpe in 1881. By 1891 they had moved to Barwick-in-Elmet and were living in The Boyle with their son John, and his family. Next door to them lived her daughter, Sarah Jane and husband Charles Parker and eight children.

By 1901 Martha was a widow and living on her own in The Boyle. She ended her days living in the Almshouses at Aberford.

Printed by Collective (UK) Limited

# The Parish of Barwick-in-Elmet

## from a map of 1819–21.

PARISH BOUNDARY ········

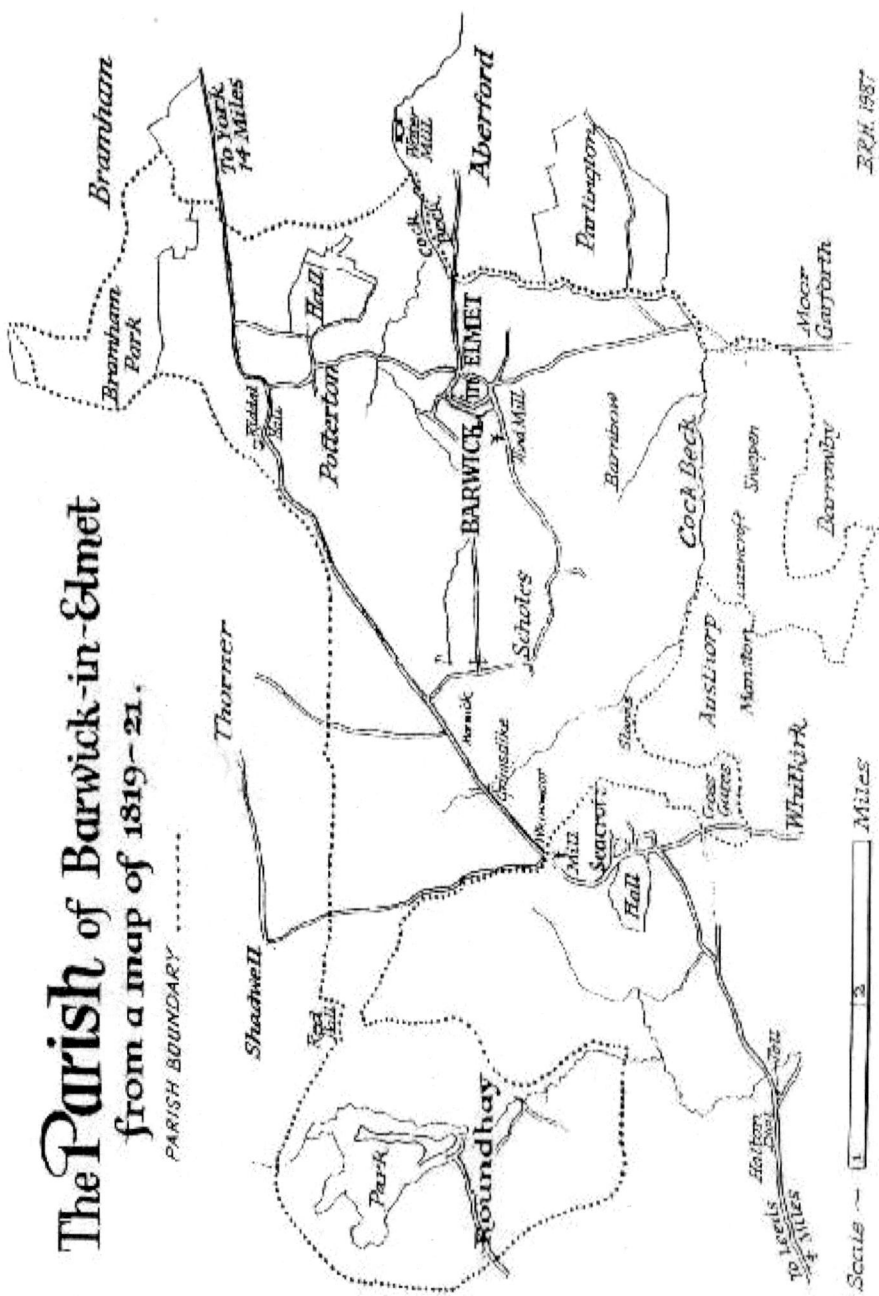

Bramham

Bramham Park

To York 14 Miles

Riddal Hall

Potterton

Hall

Cock Beck

Aberford

Parlington

BARWICK IN ELMET

Wind Mill

Moor Garforth

Thorner

Scholes

Barwick

Cock Beck

Saxton

Austhorp

Morwick

Scholecroft

Snappen

Barrowby

Shadwell

Red Hall

Barwick

Grimesdike

Penwell

Mill

Seacroft

Hall

Goose Gates

Morrows

Whitkirk

Roundhay

Park

Halton Dial

Dean

To Leeds 4½ Miles

B.P.H. 1981

SCALE — 1 | 2 | Miles

4

# BARWICK-IN-ELMET

Taken in the 1960s showing clearly how ladders were used to raise the maypole sufficiently for the ropes to take over the task.

In 1947 Dorothy Longfield was May Queen and is shown with her train bearers and children dressed for maypole dancing. Among her attendants were Pat Birch, Margaret Rowe, Pat Birdsall, Pat Murphy, Nora Dickinson, Gertie Cawston, Maureen Perry, Ann Poulter, Jennifer Nutton, and Murial Poulter.

Another photograph of Dorothy Longfield, with crown bearer, David Bowes, flanked by equerries David Lewis (left) John Murphy and Patricia Blythe.

Nellie Stead who was May Queen in 1925 with her parents John and Eva Stead who lived on The Boyle.

Rehearsing in 1931 for the Maypole ceremony.

In 1931 Margaret Bowes was crowned May Queen by Miss Nussey from Thorner.

William Osborne and his wife Catherine (née Bowes).

Catherine spent her childhood at The Gatehouse, Whinmoor, before living in Barwick. William was a widower when he married Catherine at Barwick church in 1904. They lived much of their married life in Seacroft and were buried at Barwick within four months of each other in 1926.

This picture was taken in 1957 and shows from left to right:
Tony Gilliam, Ben Strafford, Edward Poulter, Arthur Walton,
Jim Hannam and John White.

The village street with the bottom of the Maypole and the village cross.

A dray is shown outside the Black Swan.
Taken in 1910

© By kind permission of the Thoresby Society

Rectory Garden, 1901.

The May Queen and Maypole dancers. The Rector, Revd. Colman, can be seen at the left rear in a straw hat, probably carrying his daughter, Grace.

1908 The May Queen and her attendants at the Barwick Carnival.

1906 The Scholes and Barwick Carnival in Hall Tower field.

Arthur Nicholls finishing his climb of the Maypole in 1957.

Benny Strafford, Arthur Walton and Raymond Lund digging out the pole in the 1950s.

Arthur Walton and an unidentified young rider.
Probably taken at the 1966 Maypole ceremony.

Entering Barwick from Potterton showing the cottages known as 'The Limes' possibly pre-1914. Little has changed in this scene in the last 100 years.

Main Street, Barwick, in the late 1950s, just before the parade of shops was built in front of the house on the left, erroneously called The Manor House.

School photograph taken in the early 1930s.

The Headmaster, Mr Gilbert Ashworth, is shown with pupils who include, Fred Richardson, John Hague, Willie Healds, Billy Bowes, Jack Wilson and Robin Prince, Edie Oldfield, Ellen Firth, Nellie Robshaw, Annie Richardson, Mary Walton, Ivy Bullen, Emily Henderson, Doris Green, Rene Robshaw, Gertie Birch, Jack Lovett, Celia Poulter, Mary Poulter, Marian Bullen, Murial Hague, Annis Firth, Lily Lund, David Bowes, Harold Whitfield, Kenneth Speak, Dick Bell, Roy Firth.

Barwick Carnival June 1906

A class at Barwick School in 1921

Miss Garbutt, the teacher, lived at Hook Moor corner, and cycled to the school every day. Children include: Ivy Noble, Nora Lovett, Peggy Cooper, Tommy Tennant, Dougie Green, (Nurse Green's son), the two Garbutt brothers from the New Inn, Dora Howlett, Hilda Robshaw, Jackie Jaques, Joe Robshaw, two Illingworth brothers, Willy Cooper, the Green sisters from Potterton, Ernest or Willie Pawson, Stan Goodall, Alice Hudson from Rakehill Farm cottages, Dick Walton, Dorothy Nutton, and Bobby Garbutt.

The Maypole procession assembling at the school in Aberford Road in 1960, or perhaps a little earlier. 1960 was the last year that the floats were horse drawn.

Fancy dress, possibly for a Barwick Carnival, in the first decade of the twentieth century.

Potterton Lane about 1910.
Tree felling in 2008 has almost restored this view.

The Attic Abode (before nos.66-70 Main Street were built).

The two cottages were rented by Leeds artists as a weekend retreat in the 1890s and early 1900s. The cottages were next door to the village smithy.

Main Street in late Victorian times showing The 'Attic Abode' on the left. The base of the barn next door is still in use as a front wall.

The interior of the Attic Abode.

Fred Thorpe at Lime Tree Farm. The church tower is just visible on the right.

The start of Potterton Lane in the late 1950s. The house was owned by Tommy Kirk for many years.

The village centre taken in the 1940s. The man with the bicycle is Joe Balderson who was a gardener at the Rectory.

Charlie Noble on his Fordson tractor. This photograph was taken at the University Farm (Manor Farm) about 1918. This was one of the first tractors in the district.

The Miners' Welfare Institute in Chapel Lane before 1935. The building was the first Methodist Chapel in the village until 1900.

Ernest Hague, a Barwick butcher, is seen here, with his van at the Aberford Road end of Chapel Lane some time after 1945.

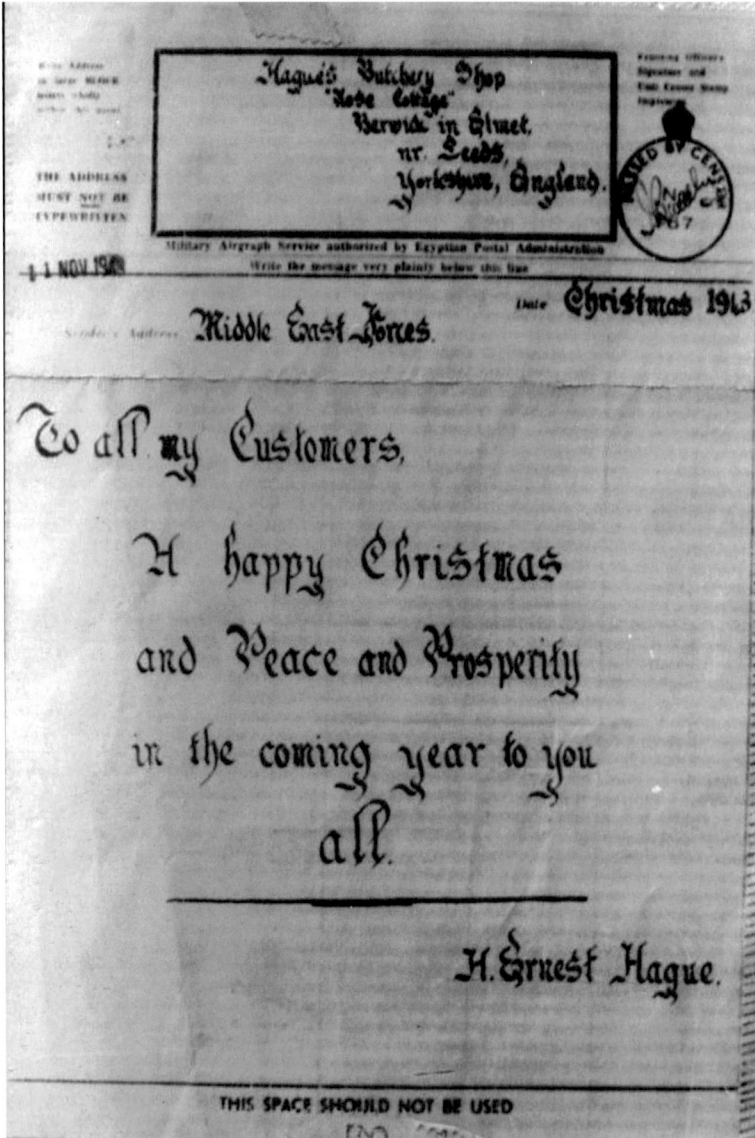

Christmas Greetings in 1943. This was sent by Ernest Hague to his old customers whilst he was away serving in the Middle East during WWII.

Fred Thorpe harvesting near the top of Flats Lane. This photograph was taken in the days before the combine harvester.

The Boyle prior to 1914. The shop on the left was the Post Office. On the right is Grove House which had been a girls' boarding school in Victorian times. The house beyond that was a cafe for cyclists.

The Fly Line from Aberford to Garforth. The train can be seen in the distance and two boys are seen sitting on the wall. The Fly Line closed in the 1920s.

Barwick Cricket Club about 1890.

Barwick Tennis Club about 1927

L-R  Connie Lumb, Leslie Collett, Winnie Haigh, Olive Collett, Denis Baker and his brother, Jack Foxcroft. Standing is Bill Lumb

Barwick Terrace is on the right going towards Scholes covering nos. 108-118 Leeds Road. This photograph was taken about 1930.

The village war memorial at some time between 1922 and 1930. The cottage behind the memorial has Threlfall's Cafe sign displayed.

The wedding of Walter Hewitt and Cecilia Balderson
in August 1915.

The bridesmaid on the left is Lucy Hewitt, the groom's sister. The bride's father, Joe, is to the left of the bride and her mother, Jeanette, is on the right of the row. Best man, Henry Poulter, is on right of back row.

The southern end of Main Street between 1963 and 1972.

The New Inn is the white building.

Barwick Darby and Joan Club in the 1950s.

The club met at the Miners' Institute. Among those attending were Mrs Ethel Hopton, landlady of the Black Swan (back row 3rd from right) Mrs Day, Mrs Freeman, Mrs Speak, Mrs Austin, Mrs Kirk, Mrs Gillian and Mrs Johnson.

Ass Bridge between Barwick and Aberford about 1930

A rare sight! Barwick in the snow during the 1990s.

Barwick Methodist Church in recent times.

The Cross, situated to the right of the Black Swan, about 1900.

This photograph was taken about 1910 showing the corner of Main Street and Leeds Road. The New Inn can be seen on the right.

Barwick School taken about 1900.

A view of Barwick Main Street. The second building on the left used to be Hewitt's butchers shop.

BARWICK FROM THE CHURCH TOWER

The west view from church tower, probably taken before 1939.

The bottom of The Boyle.

The track at the side of this cottage led to the back of 46, 48, 50 and 52 The Boyle and also to the Big House where Mr Hartley lived (landlord of the four cottages).

The interior of Barwick church taken in the early years of the 20th century.

The Oriel window at Kiddal Hall.

This photograph was taken about 1880, it shows an unidentified poorly dressed boy by the window. The window, along with the 500 year old timber ceiling and other artefacts, was sold to William Randolph Hearst in the 1920s, shipped to New York and stored for over 20 years. The window was last recorded in a sale in the 1950s, after which it was lost.

Kiddal Hall before the sale of some of its features in the 1920s.

Potterton Hall West Wing.   Date uncertain

Fire fighters practising at the Barnbow Shell Factory at Shippen
1914-1918.

BARWICK.

This picture is taken from the church looking towards the Maypole. Part
of the Methodist church can be seen in the distance.

Mill Cottages off Leeds Road. Part of the mill can be seen in the background.

Some of the cast in the pre-war Barwick Players production of 'Oliver Twist'.

Elizabeth Robshaw with garland.

She was the grand-daughter of Mrs Emmery (see front cover). The garland is considerably smaller than the ones used nowadays.

The porch at All Saints' Church, Barwick.

No. 70 Main Street.
The building replaced the Attic Abode in Edwardian times.

The Village Cross taken in 1903.

# STANKS

Looking towards Scholes, the Toll Bar on Barwick Road at Stanks was demolished in 1933. The railway bridge can be seen in the distance.

Barwick Road Stanks, looking towards Scholes, showing Windsor Terrace on the left (now Stanks Lane South).

Children playing Horses in fields at the side of Cock Beck, Stanks about 1895.

The Old School at Stanks, built in 1838.

Situated next to Windsor Terrace in Green Lane. In 1856 the school was turned into cottages. These cottages were demolished in 1953.

Watson's shop on Barwick Road, Stanks.

Taken in 1907 Watson's was a general store plus Off Licence. In the 1950s William Watson, used to walk down Pendas Way with either a duck or goose following behind him.

The photograph taken in 1896, shows children playing on a bridge over thc Cock Beck at Stanks.

This photograph was taken in the 1950s showing the building the Community Centre on Pendas Way, Stanks.

Party at Stanks Methodist Sunday School about 1947

The adults include:
Arthur Wilby (organist), Mary Meek, Miss Masterman, Margaret Meek.
Children include:
Brian Ramsden, Graham Beverley, Michael Newsom, Jean Newsom, Brenda Bosomworth, Iris Gamble, Brian Murphy, Trevor Gamble, Peter Newsom, David Masterman, Alexandra Garden, Jacqueline Meek, Pauline Bairstow, Roger Gamble, Desmond Ramsden.

Clearing snow on Barwick Road Stanks.

Taken in March 1937. Windsor Terrace is on the left. The Wetherby Line railway bridge can be seen in the distance.

PEACE DAY STANKS JULY 19ᵗʰ 1919

WWI Peace Day Celebrations at Stanks, July 1919.

The Fold, Stanks.

In the 1950s Mr Myers lived in the first cottage, the Newsam family lived in one of the other cottages. The land opposite the cottages, behind the hedge, was part of Adamson's Farm.

1907 Barwick Road, Stanks looking towards Scholes. The Toll Bar on the left is seen in front of Windsor Terrace.

Laurel Terrace, Stanks

Barwick Road, Stanks, showing Manston Manor old people's residential home now demolished and replaced with modern flats.

The Cock Beck at Whinmoor

The Paddock belonging to Adamsons Farm taken in the 1960s. When the farm was sold houses were built on the land and it became Adams Grove.

# SCHOLES

The original St Philip's Church at Scholes post 1902.

The porch has since been demolished. The group of people (bottom left) appear to be in late Victorian/ Edwardian dress.

Harvest time inside the old church of St Philip's at Scholes.

Aerial view about 1933 showing Badger Terrace at the left hand side.(The Badger being part of the family crest of the Gray family of Morwick Hall). To the rear is the Village Hall which was opened in 1931. The former Scholes Hall can be seen on the lower right hand side.

Rose Cottage, Scholes.

The former house of Tommy Walker who worked with his father Percy and brother Samuel on their Lower Barnbow market garden.The cottage was near the bend of Main Street, opposite the former Council Offices.

A winter's view of the lane leading from Scholes to Barwick, nowadays known as Rakehill Road. The bridge in the distance takes the lane over the Rake Beck.

The Coronation Tree planted in 1902.

Situated at the junction of Scholes Main Street and the road leading to Barwick. The original tree died and was replaced. It is believed that a bottle was buried near the root containing coins of the realm and two newspapers to commemorate the crowning of King Edward VIII. Mr Weatherall is shown in the front of the photograph.

Approach to Scholes Brick works on Wood Lane.

This photograph was taken in 1908. The house is flanked by the kiln and boiler house chimneys. Isaac Chippindale founded the brickworks in 1878.

View of brickworks from a bridge over the former railway line, on Wood Lane.

Isaac Murray Chippindale.

This photograph shows Isaac Murray Chippindale astride a belt driven motor cycle in front of a large stack of the bricks produced by Scholes brickworks. It was taken about 1907.

Arthur Chippindale was Isaac's elder brother. Arthur developed Arthursdale which was named after him.

Scholes Station about 1908.

The Leeds Wetherby railway line was opened in May 1876. The first station master was William Outhwaite with his family of eight children. The last station master was Donald Reed.

Scholes Station early 1960s.

The English Electric type 3N.6736 engine shown passing through. During 1961-63 Newcastle-Liverpool diesel/electric trains used this route.

The Gate Keeper's cottage on Stockheld Lane, Whinmoor, was built adjacent to the railway line. The line was closed in 1964 and the property is now a private residence.

VE Day celebration in 1945 at Scholes showing:
L-R Freda Noble, Barbara Sirrell, Sheila Hughes, Marian Overend, and Mavis Sharp.

Scholes cricket team about 1905

Scholes Lodge 1895

Taken in the Old School Yard at Scholes in 1931.

The children include:
John Townsend, Gordon Bellhouse, Raymond Froggat, Ronnie Murphy or Murfin, Reg Sirrell, Doug Froggat, Roy Sirrell, Geoff Boyce, Eric Hudson, Tony Sharp, Percy Foster, Harry Woodward, Ron Bader, Bobby Walker, Bellhouse, Jack Sirrell, Vivian Pearson, Audrey Pearson, Avril Pickford, Pauline Carr, Judy Sharp, Blanche Gader, Freda Sloan, Harry Walker, Arnold Foster, Don Hartley, Keith Henecan, Breda Carr, Dorothy Ackroyd. Lois Townend, Arnold Foster, Don Hartley, Keith Henecan, Brenda Carr and Dorothy Ackroyd.

Jane Musgrave Crosland.

Wife of John Crosland, farmer, of Scholes. The photograph was probably taken in the 1860s.

The passenger in this car is believed to be Mary Ann Arnott of Ashfield House who died in 1929. The car is a 2-seater Jowett which belonged to her nephew, Frederick, a keen photographer who purchased it in 1924 at a cost of about £70 from Harrogate Motors.

Ashfield House (7 Station Road).

The house was built in 1884 by Mary Ann Arnott, and her sister Emma and brother Frederick. This photograph was taken about 1899.

Main entrance to Barnbow National Shell Filling Factory.

Constructed in 1915 the factory, Manston Lane, Shippen occupied some 400 acres. The workforce reached 16,000 (93% female) working on 3x 8 hour shifts.

A 1907 scene of a Leeds to York Royal Mail van snowbound on the York Road near Scholes Lane, Whinmoor.

Scholes Village Players.

Taken in 1965 whilst performing 'Fool's Paradise' by Peter Coke. L-R Norah Higgins, Graham Rollinson, Linda Lancaster, Ursula Bean, Doris Ivatts, Christine Hudson.

Scholes Village Players performing 'Remember Mama' in March 1984.

Hawthorn Cottages, Whinmoor.

The Old Red Lion Inn at Whinmoor.
The public house is still standing today although it has been modernised.

# ROUNDHAY

Elmete Hall.
Once the home of the Kitson family who had major engineering works in Hunslet, Leeds.
© by kind permission of Leeds Library and Information Service,
http://www.leodis.net

Elmete Lane leading to Elmete Hall showing the stable block and clock tower.

© by kind permission of Leeds Library and Information Service,
http://www.leodis.net

The kitchen inside Elmete Lodge.

Notice the crack running down the wall and the clothes airer on the ceiling.

© by kind permission of Leeds Library and Information Service. http://www.leodis.net

Another view of the kitchen showing a further crack in the ceiling, at the opposite side of the room, running down the wall.

© by kind permission of Leeds Library and Information Service, http://www.leodis.net

The outside of Elmete Lodge.

The Elmete Hall Estate was sold by public auction on 25 July 1900. After lying empty for just over a century Elmete Hall has now been refurbished and is used as office accommodation.

# RED HALL

Red Hall, in the outer parish, was built for Richard Lodge about 1650. In the 1970s it was a nursing home for elderly people and in 1995 it was taken over by the headquarters of the Rugby League and is now used by the Leeds Parks Dept.

Part of the interior of Red Hall.